HOLIDAY of a LIFETIME

John Dougherty

Illustrated by **Robin Boyden**

OXFORD
UNIVERSITY PRESS

Families are curious things. They come in all shapes and sizes and they throw all sorts of different personalities together. And yet, oddly, lots of families seem to work pretty well.

My family never owned a camper van. We used to tow our caravan to the same caravan site every year, and stay there for a week or so. Sometimes I used to wish we had a camper and could drive off in it to have adventures, like Izzy's family in this story. I suspect, though, that – like Izzy – I might not have enjoyed the reality of life on the road, cooped up with parents and siblings who were in some ways very different from me.

And like her, when it all got too much, I'd probably have hidden myself in stories. I hope you enjoy reading this story as much as I enjoyed writing it.

John Dougherty

The Travelling Travises!

Welcome to our blog! We've set this up so our friends and family can keep up with our news over the summer holidays!

For those of you who don't know, we're about to set off on an amazing road trip! Here we are with the specially converted van that's going to be our home for the next six weeks!

We're going to have a 'vantastic' time!

The kids are *sooooo* excited. There's been such a buzz in the Travis household for the last few weeks. And we're almost ready to go! As soon as school breaks up tomorrow, we'll pick them up in the van, and head for the ferry. First stop, France!

Check back here often to see what amazing adventures we're having!

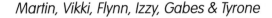

Martin, Vikki, Flynn, Izzy, Gabes & Tyrone

Chapter 1
The Van

That's my Dad's first blog post. There are three things about it that I'd like you to notice.

First: the exclamation marks. If I used half as many – no, a *quarter* as many – in a piece of homework, my teacher would hand it back to me and make me do it again. 'Izzy,' she'd say, 'there's no reason to use all those exclamation marks. If you want to make your reader feel excited, use some exciting vocabulary. And use it to describe something exciting.'

Second: the terrible joke. If you can call it a joke.

And third, and most important: I'd like you to observe that it's not quite true. Which is funny – not to mention a little hypocritical – because Dad is always impressing upon us how important it is to tell the truth.

The true bit:

We're going away on holiday. For six weeks. In a van.

The might-not-be-true bit:

'We're about to set off on an amazing road trip!' It's a road trip, but I'm not at all convinced that it's going to be amazing.

The quite-definitely-not-true bit:

'The kids are *sooooo* excited. There's been such a buzz in the Travis household for the last few weeks.'

Let's leave aside the fact that there's only one 'o' in 'so'. The kids are *not* so excited. There hasn't been a 'buzz' in the Travis household. If there's been a noise of any sort in the Travis household, it's been an irritating high-pitched whine, courtesy of my irritating little brother Tyrone. And if you look at the photo, you'll see that although all of us are doing our best to smile for the camera – except Flynn, who isn't making any effort at all – Dad's very nearly the only one who looks *really* happy.

Tell you what: let me take you back to the beginning. To the moment that Mum and Dad unleashed the horrible news upon us.

It was an ordinary Tuesday near the end of term. I'd just got home from school and was looking at my homework and wondering why I had to do it, when from outside there came this deafeningly, thunderously loud roaring noise.

'What on earth?' said my annoying little brother.

No, not Tyrone. He's my *irritating* little brother. My *annoying* little brother is Gabriel – Gabes. He's exactly a year younger than me. To the day. Which means that Mum and Dad spent the whole of my first birthday at the hospital, and ever since then I've been forced to share all my birthdays with him.

Anyway, the roaring got louder and louder, and then something big shuddered to a clumsy halt right in front of

the house. Gabes and I looked at each other and
ran outside.

There it was. A van. A big, ugly van. A really big,
really ugly van. It was probably about as big as a van can
be before you have to start calling it a truck, and it was
painted in horrible yellow, pink and green colours. And
leaning nonchalantly out of the window, looking horribly
self-satisfied ...

Dad.

Gabes and I looked at each other again. This looked
ominously like one of Dad's ideas. One of his less terrific
ideas.

'Dad,' I said cautiously, 'what's that?'

Dad grinned. 'This,' he said, 'is probably the best idea
I've ever had!'

My heart sank. Don't get me wrong – Dad's a good dad.
He's great at all the ordinary dad things – making us dinner,
tucking us in, giving us cuddles, helping with homework.
In fact, he'd be pretty much the perfect dad if he could just
stop having ideas. But every now and then he decides that
something's going to be great, and usually it isn't but we all
have to do it anyway. And if he tells us that an idea is the
best he's ever had ... Well, it's probably really, really not.

'What have you done, Dad?' I asked.

He grinned. 'Call your mum and the others, and I'll
show you.'

When Mum came down, it was obvious that she knew about the van already. She had that expression she sometimes gets, where you can tell that Dad hasn't completely persuaded her about something but she's not going to embarrass him by saying so.

'Oh,' she said, a bit too brightly. 'It's really happening, then?'

'What is?' said Flynn – my infuriating *big* brother – which was surprising for two reasons. One, because it was quite a long sentence for him; he hasn't used his voice much since it broke. Not at home, anyway. And two, because it was a response to what Mum had just said, which meant that he'd heard her, which meant that for once his headphones weren't firmly jammed on his head.

Tyrone said nothing, but just edged closer to Mum and squinted suspiciously at the van.

Dad was still grinning.

'Come on in,' he said.

We went in.

The interior of the van was ... interesting. It was kind of like being in a badly-made, overstuffed caravan. There were two tables – a little one at the back of the van and a big one at the front, just behind the driver's seat. On one side of both tables there were bench seats with lumpy-looking cushions. In the middle of the van there was a cooker, and a fridge, and a cupboard, and something that might have been a pantry or a little room – it was hard to tell with the door closed. Opposite the closed door and the small table, there was a pair of bunk beds.

It was a bit of a squeeze with all of us standing in there.

'Well?' Dad said proudly.

'My,' said Mum, her voice still a bit too bright. 'You *have* been busy, haven't you?'

The rest of us looked warily around the van. There was a pause. Then:

'What's it for?' asked Flynn suspiciously.

Dad's grin was broader than ever. 'We're going on holiday!' he said.

'In *this*?' I asked, casting an incredulous eye around the tiny space.

Dad missed the note of concern in my voice. Or maybe he pretended not to hear it. 'Yes!' he said. 'I bought it last December. It's been parked at Aunty Fi's. She helped me convert it. Isn't it great?'

I looked around the van. It didn't look great, to be honest. The lumpy cushions were stapled inelegantly on to the seats; the tables looked like we might get splinters from them; the kitchen area gave every impression of having been cobbled together from the contents of an abandoned scrapyard. So I said nothing. But Flynn didn't.

'How long?' he said.

'How long did it take us to convert it?' Dad said. 'Well, let me see … Installing the bathroom probably took a week … ' He gestured towards the closed door. 'And then the garage had to fit the seat belts … '

'No, how long are we going for?' asked Flynn, in what was probably the longest and most complicated sentence any of us had heard him utter for about two years.

Dad's grin widened. 'Six whole weeks!' he said. 'The entire summer holidays!'

Flynn spun on his heel and left the van, slamming the door behind him. A moment later, we heard the front door of the house slamming too.

Dad looked at Mum.

'Don't worry, love,' she said. 'You know what he's like at the moment. He'll come round to the idea.'

I doubted that. Knowing Flynn, he'd already made plans for the summer – mostly to do with hanging out with his friends, at a guess. Quite possibly he'd planned to go to a music festival or something as well. I couldn't see him coming round to the idea of spending the summer squashed into a van with his family.

I couldn't see *me* coming round to it either.

'Where are we going to sleep?' I asked.

Dad's grin returned, although without the same enormous helping of enthusiasm. 'It's pretty clever,' he said, 'though I do say so myself. The tables and benches convert into beds – look!'

He lifted up the corner of the cushions on one of the benches, and indicated a little ridge along the front edge of the woodwork. 'You fold the table legs down to the same height as the bench, and rest the tabletop on this ridge. Then you put the cushions from the back of the seats across the table, and hey presto: you've got a bed.'

'Right,' I said slowly. 'So you and Mum will sleep – ?'

'On the one at the front of the van,' he said. 'And then you four can sleep at the back. I thought that Flynn could have the bottom bunk and Tyrone could have the top one—'

He got no further. Tyrone's face went pink and wrinkled up. Tears started squirting from the corners of his eyes. His mouth went square, and from it came a horribly familiar and horribly irritating sound:

'eeeee**eeeeee!**'

Dad panicked. When Tyrone starts howling – which he does a *lot* – it's practically impossible to get him to stop.

'Hey, bud! What's wrong?'

'I don't – *eeeee* – I don't wanna – *eeeee* – I don't *wanna* sleep on the top bunk! eeee**eeeeeee!**'

Dad picked him up and wiped his face. 'Hey,' he soothed. 'Hey – it's OK! You don't have to sleep on the top bunk if you don't want to. It was just an idea. Would you rather sleep on the bottom bunk?'

Tyrone sniffled. The howling softened to a whimper and he nodded slowly.

'There we go,' Dad said. 'That was easy.'

'So what about the rest of us?' I asked cautiously.

'Well,' Dad said, 'Flynn will never fit in the top bunk. So I guess Gabes could go in the top one and you could go in the double bed with Flynn—'

'No!' I almost yelled. 'Sorry, Dad, but I'm *not* sharing a bed with Flynn! He's big and smelly and—'

I could see that Dad was going to argue, but luckily Mum butted in. Gently, but firmly, she said, 'Izzy's right, love.'

Dad opened his mouth to argue, and then closed it again. 'OK,' he said, contemplating first me and then the top bunk. 'Izzy could fit in the top one. So that means Gabes and Flynn sharing the bed. Sorted!'

'Flynn's never going to want to share a bed with Gabes,' I pointed out. 'Not with any of us, for that matter. He's never going to go for it.'

I waited for Gabes to back me up. I mean, it was obvious that Dad's plan was a recipe for disaster. All of us, cooped up together in a space as cramped and confined as this one for the whole summer? It'd drive us mad! So I looked at my annoying little brother and waited for him to agree. Then Dad would have to admit that the plan was hopeless.

Gabes looked back at me and smiled. And then he said ...

I still can't believe it.

He said, 'That's OK. I can sleep in the front.'

'But Gabes,' said Dad, 'that's where your mum and I are sleeping.'

'No, Dad,' Gabes said. 'I mean the very front row of seats, where the driver sits. We can turn that into a bed for me. I'll be just in front of you and mum.'

Dad grinned. 'Gabes,' he said, 'you're a genius.'

Gabes grinned back, and I swear that for a moment he looked just like a miniature replica of Dad. I scowled at my annoying little brother, hoping the sheer intensity of my glare would make his head explode.

It didn't.

Honestly, he could so easily have finished Dad's plan off there and then. Instead, he'd condemned us to six weeks crammed together in this van with Flynn being grumpy and Tyrone howling and Gabes being annoying and Dad trying to persuade us all we were having a great time. This was going to be awful.

The Travelling Travises!

What a fantastic start to our holiday! So far, everything's run pretty smoothly – OK, there've been one or two hiccups, but nobody's perfect, eh?

Overall, though, it's been great! We arrived in plenty of time for the ferry – which Tyrone loved! I think he'd have been happy if we'd spent the whole holiday on board!

The ferry crossing was pretty smooth – though poor old Gabes felt a bit queasy on the way across! Still, we got to France all in one piece. Now we're camped for the night – and, hey! I've got a phone signal! So this is just a quick blog post to let all our friends know we're here and raring to go. More soon!

Martin, Vikki, Flynn, Izzy, Gabes & Tyrone

Chapter 2
The Ferry

Well, that's one way of looking at it.

Or rather, that's *Dad's* way of looking at it. Someone really ought to have a word with him about his blog.

I mean, look at what he said about the ferry. 'Poor old Gabes felt a bit queasy on the way across!'

'A bit queasy'? That's like saying that Einstein was a bit clever, or the sea is a bit wet, or the stars are a bit far away. Gabes was not just 'a bit queasy'; he was horribly, wretchedly seasick. He went green almost the moment we left the dock.

Not that I felt sorry for him. If it hadn't been for Gabes, we wouldn't have been on the ferry in the first place, with that nightmare of a converted van lurking below deck like a ghastly motorized Frankenstein's monster. Besides, who do you think had to stay with him?

That's right. Me.

It was my own fault, really. I should have done what Flynn did, which was to disappear the moment we got on board and not show my face again till it was time to go back to the monstrosity on wheels. But no; I had to go and see what was happening.

Well, all right; really, I wanted to enjoy the sight of my annoying little brother suffering. He'd been intolerable ever since Dad had brought the van home, going on about where he wanted to go, and what he wanted to see, and how much fun it was going to be. But of course as soon as I got near, Dad said, 'Oh, Izzy. Can you keep Gabes company for a while? He's feeling a bit poorly.' And before I could respond, he'd scarpered, leaving me alone with my nauseous and nauseating brother.

* * *

There was silence, except for the whipping of the briny wind around my face, and the lamentations of the seagulls that hung above us like lonely ghosts, and the wretched sounds of Gabes being sick.

To pass the time, I thought about how I was going to describe this scene when I wrote it down. I'd already decided to keep a journal of our holiday – I want to be a writer, you see, and I think it's important to get a lot of practice in now. I got out my phone and used my thesaurus app to help me find words to describe the rest of the scene. I decided the seagulls' cries sounded like 'lamentations'. I nearly went for 'ululations', because it almost sounds as if they're going 'ul ul ul ul ul', but I thought more people would know what 'lamentations' meant. I made a real effort to remember 'ululation', though. You can never have too many words for 'crying' when you're a writer with a brother like Tyrone.

Dad came back when we were about halfway across and offered to swap with me, but Tyrone went 'eeeeeeeeeeee!' and when Dad did his whole 'Hey, mate! What's wrong?' routine, he ululated, 'I wanna – *eeeee* – I wanna – *eeeeee* – I wanna stay with *you*!'

I have no idea where Mum was. Probably lying down somewhere, or in the cafe with a nice cup of tea, enjoying the peace and quiet while she could.

* * *

At last the crossing was over. The ferry docked and we made our way down to the car decks. It was supposed to be my turn to sit in the front with Mum and Dad, but Mum said Gabes had to sit there in case he felt sick again.

The engines started, and the cars in front of us rolled off. For one horrid moment it looked as if our van wasn't going to start, but then it did, and we eased forward, along the car deck and down the ramp.

'We're in France, everyone!' said Dad, a bit too cheerily. 'The holiday starts here!'

'Yay!' said Mum feebly.

Nobody else said anything. Flynn was sitting next to me, headphones on and eyes closed. Tyrone was glued to a little DVD player. The only sounds were the spluttering of the engine, and Gabes coughing into a paper bag.

Chapter 3
The Meadow

We stopped for lunch at the first motorway services we came to. Flynn complained that there wasn't enough on his plate, but then he got another helping, since Tyrone insisted on getting something and then discovered he wasn't hungry.

As soon as we could, we set off again; and we drove and drove and drove. Dad kept chattering about all the fun things we were going to see and do, and Mum kept joining in, but nobody else said very much. Well, except for Gabes, once he started to feel better. He kept asking stupid questions: Were we going to see any mountains? Would we go swimming in the sea? And, of course, did Mum and Dad think there would be any unusual animals?

Gabes wants to be a zoologist when he grows up. Everything about animals fascinates him: the way they look, the way they move, their eating habits, their sleeping habits, what they look like when they're dead, their bones ... You could go as far as to say he's completely obsessed with them. It's all he ever thinks about.

Anyway, the next few hours were spent on the road, which was an utterly tedious experience. It was late afternoon when Mum suggested, 'Should we find somewhere to camp for the night, everyone?'

And then we spent another hour looking for a campsite, or a lay-by, or something. It appeared that neither Mum nor Dad had given any thought at all to the rather important point that it's no use having a van to sleep in unless there's somewhere you can stop the van and go to sleep.

Eventually, Dad spotted an open gate leading to a wide track. 'How about this?'

Mum looked worried. 'I don't know, Martin. Isn't it likely to be a farm or something?'

Dad shook his head. He looked pretty fatigued. 'I think it's probably public land. If it was a farm, the gate would be closed.'

For a moment I thought Mum was going to argue – she hates breaking rules – but then Dad yawned, a great big exhausted yawn, and she put her hand on his arm and said, 'All right, then. If you're sure.'

Dad turned the van off the road and we drove up the track, through a thick covering of trees, and into a wide overgrown meadow.

'How's this?' Dad asked, pulling up and switching off the engine.

I hadn't realized how stuffy it felt in the van until we opened the door and a crisp, fresh summer breeze swept in to meet us. We clambered out into the evening sunshine, stretching our travel-stiffened limbs.

'First night's camping!' said Dad. 'Shall we have a campfire?'

'I don't think so, love,' Mum said. I could tell she was still concerned we might be trespassing. 'We ought to have an early night. We're all pretty tired.'

'Can I go and play?' Tyrone asked.

'Don't wander off,' Mum told him. 'And that goes for all of you. I'll get some food ready.'

I strolled around the meadow for a while, enjoying the evening. The slowly sinking sun cast dappled shadows through the trees; the grass, ruffled by the gentle breeze, stroked my bare shins. In the trees, birds were singing. From somewhere nearby, I could hear the sound of a river.

Not far from the van, bathed in sunlight, stood a fragment of wall – now no more than a collection of stones, but once, perhaps, a boundary, or a portion of a building. I put my hand out and touched it; it was warm, having soaked up the sun's heat all day.

I'm fascinated by historical artefacts. I like to imagine that very old things absorb all the history they're steeped in, and that when you touch them you're connecting with all the lives that have been there before you. So I stood there, eyes closed, hand on the wall, imagining that it had once been part of a great manor house which had been burned down during the French Revolution. I pictured the great lords and ladies who lived there being captured and taken off to Paris to be executed. And I was just beginning to make up a story involving a serving girl of about my age, who set out to rescue her employers from the revolutionaries, when—

'Look at that!'

It was Gabes. Absolutely typical of him to interrupt my flow of thought. I opened my eyes crossly and looked to see what he was pointing at.

For a minute, all I could see was stones. Stones, and moss, and lichen. And then something blinked, and I saw it. A lizard, clinging to the wall and basking in the sun's warmth.

It was amazing. I'd never seen a lizard before. I mean – I'd seen big lizards, in the zoo, but that's not the same thing. You expect to see strange creatures at the zoo; that's why you go there. But this was just a little one, resting on the wall as if it was the most natural thing in the world.

And then something moved, further along the wall, and I saw another one, and another. Gabes saw them too.

'There's loads of them!' he whispered.

I wanted to stay and look at the lizards. They looked so ... not pretty; that's the wrong word. I'm not sure 'cute' is right, either. But for whatever reason, I liked them. There was something mesmerizing about them, and about the evening sunlight and the grass and the breeze; something that made me just want to be there, to remain, standing by the wall, looking at the lizards.

Then I looked at Gabes and my state of tranquillity disintegrated, to be replaced by a feeling of sheer exasperation.

It was all very well standing in fields looking at lizards, but it didn't change the fact that I was going to have to spend the rest of the summer crammed into a van with him and Flynn and Tyrone, when I could have been at home. And it was all his fault.

I turned on my heel and marched back to the van.

The rest of the evening went much as you might imagine. After we'd eaten, we went for a walk around the meadow together and my family behaved exactly as you'd expect my family to behave.

Dad kept pointing at the view and saying how amazing it was.

Mum kept smiling and saying, 'Well – isn't this nice?' as if she thought that eventually someone would feel obliged to say, 'Yes, it's utterly lovely.' Nobody did.

Flynn kept his headphones on and his hands in his pockets, and grumpily trailed as far behind us as Dad would tolerate.

Gabes kept running off to look for lizards.

Tyrone kept looking for things to cry about. At least, that's what it seemed like.

And me? I kept wondering if I could persuade my friend Sophia's mum to adopt me when I got home.

Maybe it was all the travelling, maybe it was the hour change, but we were all pretty weary by the time we got back to the van. Even Flynn didn't grumble *too* much about having to go to bed so early. We got into our pyjamas while Dad transformed the tables into beds and Mum made us hot chocolate.

'All done!' Dad said with a smile, as we finished our drinks. 'Sure you don't mind being the one sleeping at the front, Gabes?'

'I don't mind,' said Gabes, all too cheerfully. 'It was my idea, anyway.'

That's not something to boast about, I thought. *If it hadn't been for your stupid idea, we wouldn't be here.*

We all got into bed. Mum turned the lights out, and I lay there in the dark, wondering if selling my brothers online might be an option.

* * *

We all woke fairly early the next morning, except for Flynn. He was still snoring like a rhinoceros with a chest infection when the rest of us were up, dressed, and helping with breakfast. It seemed that nothing could disturb him – clattering crockery, the shrieking whistle of the kettle, even Dad's singing. Of course, the moment the food was on the table, there he suddenly was, grunting and eating the breakfast that the rest of us had prepared.

And then it was time to go. We washed up and packed everything safely away, and buckled ourselves in as Dad started the engine. Down the track we went, through the trees ... and stopped.

'Oh,' said Dad.

The gate was closed. And dangling from it we could see a huge gleaming padlock.

'Maybe it's not actually locked,' Mum said hopefully, and hopped out of the van.

Moments later, Mum was turning to us and shaking her head theatrically.

We all got out to join her. Well, all except Flynn, who was sitting back with his eyes closed and his headphones on.

'What do we do?' said Dad.

I could see that Mum wanted to say something like: 'You tell me. You're the one who thought it was public land.' But she resisted the temptation, and instead just said weakly, 'I don't know.'

'Are we locked in?' said Gabes.

'eeeee**eeeeee!**' went Tyrone.

Dad scooped him up. 'It's OK, bud. It's OK. We'll sort this.'

It occurred to me that if we just let Tyrone go on crying, someone would be bound to hear eventually, and they'd come and rescue us; but I didn't think Mum and Dad would appreciate my saying so.

'Hey, Tyrone,' said Gabes. 'Want to come and look at the lizards?'

Tyrone didn't actually stop *crying*, but he stopped wailing inconsolably, or at least moderated it to merely wailing consolably.

'They're really cool,' Gabes added persuasively.

Still snivelling, Tyrone looked at Dad, who nodded encouragingly. 'You go with Gabes, mate. We'll call you when we're ready to go.'

Dad put Tyrone down, patting him reassuringly on the head, and after a moment, Tyrone, continuing to gulp and gasp, followed Gabes back up the track.

'So what *do* we do?' I asked.

Mum and Dad gazed at the padlock, as if hoping they might suddenly develop mysterious telekinetic abilities that would enable them to spring it open with the power of their minds.

'I don't suppose you know how to pick locks?' Dad said wryly.

Mum gave a dry laugh. 'Didn't I ever tell you about my secret life as a cat burglar?'

They carried on staring at the lock for a bit.

'Maybe we could call the police?' Mum offered.

Dad shook his head. 'I don't know,' he said. 'They might charge us with wasting police time.'

'Or trespassing,' I pointed out.

Dad had the good grace to look slightly guilty.

'Maybe there's another gate,' I offered.

It took them a moment or two to realize what I'd said.

'You know,' said Mum, 'that's not a bad suggestion.'

'It's worth a try,' agreed Dad. 'Let's go and look.'

Mum waited by the gate in case Gabes and Tyrone came back – or in case someone with a key happened along – and Dad and I walked the roadside stretch of the perimeter, along the barbed wire fence, negotiating hedges and brambles and cowpats and the occasional unexpected puddle. It took us about half an hour before we got to a place where the fence veered sharply away from the road and uphill. There was no gate.

'Any luck?' Mum asked on our return. We shook our heads gloomily. 'Well, maybe there'll be something in the other direction. Your turn to wait here, Martin.'

There wasn't anything in the other direction, except for more hedges and brambles and cowpats and puddles. I ended up with a wet shoe and Mum ended up with a smelly one.

When we returned, Dad was playing some kind of daft game with Gabes and Tyrone, and the gate was still firmly locked.

'No joy?'

Mum shook her head.

Dad scratched his chin. 'I don't think there's anything else we can do, then,' he said. 'We're going to have to call the police, and take what comes.'

'Will we be in trouble?' Gabes asked.

'eeeee**eeeeee!**' went Tyrone.

'What's going on?' said Flynn, finally emerging from the van. Nobody answered him. Mum and Dad were too busy comforting Tyrone, Tyrone was too busy going '*eeeee*', Gabes was lost in thought, and I didn't see why it was my job to explain things.

Flynn didn't seem bothered by the lack of acknowledgement. He looked at the gate, grunted, and went back inside the van.

Moments later he reappeared, holding a pair of pliers, and approached the gate.

'Flynn?' Mum said worriedly. 'What are you doing?'

Flynn ignored her. He crouched down and untwisted the ends of the barbed wire fence from the wooden gatepost. Then he took careful hold of the top strand of wire, keeping his fingers well clear of the barbs, and pulled it out of the van's way.

'Are you two going to help, or what?' he asked, looking at me and Gabes in a way I could almost have sworn had something playful about it.

It took us both a moment to react. Then we rushed over and followed his lead.

'Careful!' said Mum.

'Not you, mate,' said Dad, scooping Tyrone up as he too made a dash for the fence.

'eeeee*eeeeee!*' went Tyrone. 'I – *eeeee* – I – *eeeeee* – I* wanna help too! eeee*eeeeee!*'

'Oh, you can,' Dad assured him, carrying him towards the van and climbing in. 'I've got a *really* important job for you. I need you to look out of the window and check that we don't bump the gate on the way out. Can you do that?'

Tyrone's answer was lost in the sound of the engine starting up.

With the barbed wire peeled back, the van squeezed through the gap between the fence posts with millimetres to spare. Flynn carefully reattached the wires leaving the fence almost as good as new.

'Flynn, you're a genius,' said Dad, as he put the van in gear and released the handbrake. 'In fact, I'd go as far as to say that you're nearly as clever as your father!'

Nobody laughed. Particularly not Flynn, who was already sitting back in his seat, headphones on and eyes closed, listening to something repetitive, percussive, and – from where I was sitting – extremely irritating, like a mosquito drumming on a tiny drum kit made of tinfoil.

Off we set again, still only on day two of our holiday, and all ready for the next catastrophe.

Just kidding. We weren't ready at all.

The Travelling Travises!

We've just stopped off at a little place called St Boulet for some routine maintenance. We're really enjoying our taste of the rural French life here! And the locals are so friendly! Mustn't get too comfy, though – we'll be back on the road tomorrow!

Martin, Vikki, Flynn, Izzy, Gabes & Tyrone

Chapter 4
The Lizard

So, this 'routine maintenance'? Dad's definition of 'routine' is clearly different from the one in the dictionary. Here's what happened the next day.

We'd managed to find a supermarket along the way – an absolutely huge supermarket, actually. You could get lost in it, and, of course, Tyrone did. But that aside, it was fairly uneventful and left us with a full fridge including, among other things, everything we needed for a picnic. Mum was driving the van that morning, and had found us a pretty good picnic spot on top of a hill looking down over a little lake. There was a tree for me to climb and a little stream for Tyrone to paddle in, and Gabes found some more lizards sunning themselves on a rock. The picnic was pretty good too. All in all, it wasn't a complete disaster.

After lunch, we got back into the van and Dad took the wheel again. Tyrone, miraculously, hadn't cried once during the picnic; Gabes was looking very pleased with himself for some reason; and even Flynn had almost smiled. It probably counted as a success, overall.

After a bit, I think I dozed off for a few minutes. The last thing I remember as I closed my eyes was Gabes, holding his hands together and speaking softly into them.

The first thing I saw when I opened them again was Gabes, hysterically searching for something – checking his pockets; under the cushions; on the floor ... For a moment, I wondered what he'd lost.

Then I looked up, and I saw it. A lizard. A lizard, clinging to the ceiling of the van.

I must still have been a bit groggy, because for a moment I found myself thinking, *How did that get there?* But I worked it out almost instantaneously. Somehow – I still have no idea how – Gabes must have enticed one of the lizards from the picnic site into his hands, and decided to keep it as a pet. He must have smuggled it on board the van; Mum would have had hysterics if she'd seen him bringing an animal inside.

I stared at the lizard. It stared back at me. Then it began to move. It scooted from one side of the ceiling to the other, unable to find any cover. Panicking, it darted towards the window and scuttled down it; then back up again, and across the ceiling once more.

And then it scuttled towards the front of the van.

Wide-eyed, Gabes looked frantically at the lizard, as if willing it to come back. 'Lizzie! Lizzie!' he whispered urgently. I rolled my eyes scornfully; surely he didn't expect it to answer.

Flynn had seen it, too. He was watching with curious amusement as the lizard skittered and scurried, zigzagging across the ceiling, until it was perched right above Dad's head.

I don't know exactly what happened next. I guess the van must have hit a bump in the road. In any case, there was a jolt. The lizard dropped from the ceiling on to Dad's head. It scurried down his neck and into the darkness of his shirt.

Dad yelled in fright and jerked the wheel. There was a bump; a loud bang. We found ourselves flung forward as the van slammed to a halt.

The engine cut out, dead. Then there was silence.

Chapter 5
The Accident

The silence lasted for a mere five seconds, if that. It took six or seven for the entirely predictable 'eeeee**eeeee**!' to begin, but by that point Mum was shouting, 'Is everyone all right? Flynn? Izzy? Gabes?' and Dad had thrown himself out of the cab and was dancing around on the road, shrieking and yelling and wriggling out of his shirt.

'We're fine, Mum,' Flynn called, unbuckling his seat belt and scrambling from the van. Gabes and I followed, and Mum and Tyrone clambered out after us. Dad was flapping his shirt around with one hand and frantically brushing himself down with the other. Of the unfortunate lizard there was no sign.

Dad finally stopped yelping and leaping about and stood there, red-faced and panting. 'Did anyone see what it was?'

'What *what* was?' Mum said impatiently. 'Hush, Tyrone,' she added, so brusquely that Tyrone hushed in astonishment.

'Something attacked me,' Dad wheezed. 'Some kind of creature. Jumped on me. Ran down my shirt.'

Mum's forehead wrinkled disbelievingly. 'Really? Are you *sure*?'

'Of course I'm sure—' Dad began, but Mum interrupted.

'Anyway, never mind that now. What are we going to do? As if yesterday's escapade with the locked gate wasn't enough – '

She looked at the van. We all did.

In a way, we'd had a lucky escape. We'd come very close to leaving the road altogether and plummeting down a slope into a field. Seat belts or not, we could have been badly hurt.

Less luckily, the thing that had stopped us leaving the road was a large tree, and the bonnet of the van was now folded around its trunk.

Dad's face fell. 'Oh,' he said.

'Yes,' agreed Mum. 'Oh.'

'Well, it wasn't *my* fault—' Dad began defensively.

'Never mind whose fault it is,' Mum said sharply. 'What do we do now?'

'We'll have to phone for help,' Dad said. 'Oh,' he added, looking at his phone. 'No reception.'

'Me neither,' said Mum, looking at her own. 'Flynn?'

Flynn pulled out his phone, checked it, and shook his head.

'Great,' said Mum. 'That's just great.'

'Aw, cheer up, love,' said Dad, and then shut up as he saw the look that Mum was giving him.

After a moment he tried again. 'Look – we'll just wave somebody down and ask for help.'

'You don't speak French,' Mum reminded him.

Dad shrugged optimistically. 'I did a bit of French at school,' he said. 'I've been brushing up on it. And anyway, lots of French people speak English. It'll be fine.'

It was not fine. I dare say that if we'd broken down on some sort of busy city highway, within minutes a helpful passer-by would have stopped and engaged us in fluent English, but this was a remote rural road. It was half an hour before anybody came by – an elderly, wizened woman in a tiny little car that looked as ancient as she did.

Dad waved frantically as she approached, and she stopped and wound down the window.

Dad bent down. 'Bonjour, Madame,' he said, and then launched into a stream of what sounded very like ... well, French, actually. Honestly, it was pretty impressive. I hadn't a clue what he was saying, but it was clear that he really had been working hard on bringing his French up to scratch for the holiday.

The woman listened intently until Dad reached the end of his explanation. Then she fixed him with her bright little eyes.

'Kwa?' she said – or, at least, that was what it sounded like. It was clear that she hadn't understood a word.

'Um ... we've had an accident,' Dad tried. 'Ac-ci-d-ent?'

The woman stared at Dad for a moment, as if trying to work out exactly what he was, and then wound the window up and drove away.

Mum stared at Dad too. 'Well, that went well, didn't it?' she said. It's never a good sign when Mum gets sarcastic.

Dad frowned. 'Maybe her hearing isn't so good,' he said. 'I'm sure the next one will understand.'

The next one didn't. Nor the one after that. Nor the one after that. After that one, Dad abandoned any attempt to speak in French, but it soon became clear that in this particular part of France, nobody either possessed the ability to help us or spoke English. They may have been making helpful suggestions, but we just didn't understand them. Some of them didn't even stop. One or two pulled up, got out, examined the damage, shrugged, made a noise that sounded like 'Bof!' and left.

Eventually Mum had the bright idea of getting me to do the talking, on the assumption that people would find it more difficult to drive away from an angelic-looking child in difficulty.

So with Mum hovering nearby, I stood at the side of the road, near our poor wounded hippopotamus of a van, and waited for the next vehicle to appear, watching as the golden light of the late afternoon shone through the dappling leaves of the tall trees that lined the road.

The sun was sinking low by the time someone else arrived – a weather-beaten man of about Dad's age. He wound down the window of his old and battered pickup truck and listened carefully as I explained slowly and clearly what had happened. Then, when I'd given him as much detail as I could about the accident and the fact that we were stranded, he gazed at me seriously and said, 'Kwa?'

I could almost feel the tension crackling between Mum and Dad behind me at that moment, like an electrical storm about to break. I reckoned that if one more potential rescuer drove away, I'd hear Mum say a lot of words she normally pretends she doesn't know. At high volume.

In desperation I pointed at the front of the van, where the bonnet had crumpled around the tree, pointed at Dad and Mum, shrugged, and made a noise like 'Bof!' I guessed that was sort of French for 'I haven't a clue what to do,' and that maybe if I pointed at my parents first it would translate as '*They* haven't a clue what to do.'

The man nodded wisely. 'Ah,' he said. He got out of the pickup; walked purposefully over to the van; examined the damage closely and from several angles; scratched his chin thoughtfully and examined the damage again. He turned to me, said something in French, and made an incomprehensible gesture.

Then he got back in his truck and drove away.

At that point, I thought I'd go and see what the boys were doing. Or, rather, I thought I'd pretend to do that, in order to get out of the way before the explosion came. As I closed the van door behind me, I could hear the argument starting.

Gabes looked up from the card game he and Tyrone were involved in. 'Hi, Izzy! Want to play?'

I didn't – not with him, anyway. First he'd got us into this mess of a holiday and now he'd got us stranded by the side of the road miles from anywhere. Frankly, I didn't care for his company right then. So I flopped down next to Flynn – who was, unsurprisingly, lying back with his eyes closed and his headphones on – and took out my book.

I was only a chapter or so further along when I became aware of a noise. A loud, rumbling noise, coming closer and closer. I looked up. So did Gabes and Tyrone and, after a moment, even Flynn heard it and pulled off his headphones. We glanced at one another, rushed to the door and emptied ourselves out of the van.

It was a tractor – the biggest tractor any of us had ever seen. Down the road it trundled, like a mighty dinosaur of the highways. And behind it came a small squadron of other vehicles – three cars and two pickup trucks. As the tractor grumbled past us, the driver nodded, and I recognized the weather-beaten man.

The cars and pickups stopped before they reached us, and disgorged their drivers and passengers – mostly men, but one or two women as well. One of them opened the door of our van and gestured to Dad to get in, while the others braced themselves against the bonnet. Meanwhile, the tractor – which had found somewhere to turn, not far down the road – rumbled past us again and drew to a stop.

The assembled people began to push and slowly, slowly, the van edged backwards on to the road. Meanwhile, the first man had hopped down from the tractor with a length of strong, sturdy rope.

It didn't take long to attach the van to the tractor. In we scrambled; the enormous wheels of the great agricultural machine turned; the rope tautened. With a jerk, we began to move.

'Where are we going?' Gabes wanted to know.

'Yes, good question,' said Mum pointedly. 'Where *are* we going?'

It wasn't long before we found out. The tractor towed us into a village, past a modest sign which said 'St Boulet', and took a right turn into the forecourt of what turned out to be a garage.

The next few minutes were all confusion. Despite what Dad had originally said, no one here spoke much English, and none of us spoke any French (unless you counted Dad, which none of us – and especially not the French people – did). The mechanic tried to lock the van in the workshop; Dad tried to explain to him that we needed to sleep in it; the mechanic didn't understand, and got cross when Dad stopped him from closing the doors ...

There followed several minutes of uncertainty, topped with a big dollop of bewilderment, as Dad tried to make the villagers see that we really needed to sleep in the van while Mum tried to find out if there was anywhere else we could stay. Unfortunately, both of them were so wound up that they kept speaking quicker and quicker, and talking over each other, while several of the others made what I can only assume were helpful suggestions in French. Eventually, though, it became clear that there were rooms above the village cafe, and that we could probably rent those for as long as it would take to fix the van, so we grabbed our overnight things and went to the cafe, where it became equally clear that Dad was expected to buy refreshments for everybody who'd come to help us.

It turned out there was only one room left, so we spent the night squashed into a space that was smaller than the van and woke the next morning feeling grumpy. As soon as we'd had breakfast, Dad hurried us to the garage where, he said, we'd find the mechanic already hard at work on our van.

And that was when we discovered that, it being Sunday, the garage was closed for the day.

The Travelling Travises!

And we're back on the road at last! We spent a little longer in St Boulet than we'd planned, but none of us really minded – it's such a great little place! Still, in the end we had to say goodbye to our new friends and hit the road! Next stop – Switzerland! We're planning to do a bit of hiking in the mountains!

Martin, Vikki, Flynn, Izzy, Gabes & Tyrone

Chapter 6
The Mountain

We ended up spending a week in St Boulet. A whole week. The mechanic had to send off for some of the parts he needed to fix the van, and they didn't arrive for ages.

It could have been worse, I suppose. The sun shone every day, for one thing. Dad and Mum insisted on taking us for walks, which weren't as awful as you might have expected – though it sickened me a bit to see how Gabes leaped out of bed every morning, full of enthusiasm, as if it wasn't his fault we were stuck here. Double his fault, really – if he hadn't come up with that stupid idea about the sleeping arrangements, the whole wretched holiday would never have got off the ground, and if he hadn't gone around kidnapping lizards and dragging them away from their natural environment, we wouldn't have got ourselves stranded in St Boulet. What was worse, he owned up to the business with the lizard and – aside from a brief lecture about leaving animals where you find them – Mum and Dad forgave him! Anyway, we spent the week exploring the area – walks in the forest, swimming in the lake, that sort of thing. And finally, the van was ready and we could go.

Switzerland wasn't exactly the next stop – we visited a couple of cities and a handful of more remote spots on the way down, because Mum and Dad wanted to look at some cathedrals and castles and that sort of thing. But eventually we made it to Switzerland and headed for the Swiss Alps.

The scenery was spectacular up there – picturesque alpine villages; lush green valleys lying lazily below us; snow-capped peaks soaring majestically above us – even Flynn took time out from his headphones to enjoy the views. We went to the highest railway station in Europe, and we did a couple of trips on a cogwheel train, which is a type of train designed to go up steep inclines. We visited a mountain where they once filmed an action movie, and saw an exhibition about it – Flynn got almost enthusiastic at one point. We went to a chocolate museum, which Tyrone loved. We went to a viewing platform over a precipice, which Tyrone didn't love. We went on a revolving cable car, and visited a glacier. It almost made up for having to be squashed into that horrible van with the rest of my family.

And on our last day in Switzerland, we went on an alpine walk.

I wasn't keen on the idea – I felt we'd been on enough walks when we were stuck in St Boulet. Neither was Flynn. But when we complained, Dad said we'd vote on it.

You can probably guess what happened. Flynn and I voted against. Mum and Dad voted for. Tyrone voted for, because he was scared that if he voted against, Mum and

Dad would go anyway and leave him behind – as if *that's* ever happened.

And of course Gabes voted for the walk. With a smile on his face. Landing us all in a mess once again.

It was an absolutely gorgeous day. The sky was sapphire blue; the dazzling sun shone down like a celestial chariot riding high over the snow-capped peaks; the air was fresh and invigorating. I ran up the track to the first viewing point, unable to stop myself from smiling.

It became progressively easier to stop myself from smiling from that point on, though. First of all, while I was gazing back down at the van – already so far below us, in a parking spot on the edge of a pine forest – I found Gabes at my shoulder.

'Cool, huh?' he said, in a way that I found tremendously irritating. It was as if ... well, honestly, it was as if he thought we were friends or something. And I was *not* his friend. I was not going to forget that he'd landed us all on this stupid holiday. I was not going to forget that he'd stranded us in St Boulet for a week. And even though this walk wasn't turning out to be as bad as it might have been, I was not going to forget that it was his fault we were on it. So I just grunted and went to look at something else.

What was worse, he kept at it. Everything we saw, every new bit of trail, there was Gabes at my shoulder trying to be amiable. It got so that I couldn't enjoy the views, or the walk, or even the picnic by the waterfall – and it was an amazing waterfall. A sparkling clear river tumbling down from above, cascading over the rocky mountainside and sending a mist of fine droplets into the air around it. By rights I should have been wonderstruck just looking at it, but I felt so resentful of Gabes, and his cheeriness, and his spoiling everything and never facing the consequences, that it felt like there was a thundercloud around my heart and I couldn't enjoy anything.

Still, it was a beautiful place for a picnic – if your day wasn't being ruined by an annoying little brother trying to strike up conversations.

'Look at the way the sunlight sparkles on the waterfall, Izzy!'

'Hey, Izzy, isn't this an amazing place for a picnic?'

'Izzy! Look! I've found an alpine newt!'

We finished lunch and tidied everything away, and then Mum said, 'Right, you lot – have a good afternoon!'

'What?' I said. 'Aren't you coming back to the van with us?'

Mum laughed. '*I'm* going back to the van with Tyrone – I think he's had enough. But I'm not going to stop you lot from reaching the top of the waterfall.'

'eeeee**eeeeee**!'

'Hey! Hey, mate! What's wrong?'

'I – *eeeee* – I – *eeeeeee* – I don't wanna go back to the van!'

'OK, bud, OK! You can come with us if you want! We're going up there!' Dad pointed to the top of the waterfall.

Lip trembling, Tyrone stared up at the huge and distant lip of rock from which gallons of roaring water gushed, second by second. Then:

'eeeee**eeeeee**!'

After lengthy negotiations, Tyrone wetly and noisily agreed that going back down the mountain with Mum was preferable to continuing up the mountain with Dad and the rest of us, especially when the option of a colouring book and a DVD was added to the equation.

Then we had to explain the whole thing again to Flynn who, thanks to his headphones, had missed the entire conversation.

'Aren't we *all* going back?' he protested, treating us to one of his rare sentences.

'You're welcome to come with us, love,' Mum said, 'but I've already promised Tyrone he can choose the movie. And you're not really into the same sort of thing as he is.'

So Mum and Tyrone set off down the trail again, back to the van, while Dad led a grumpy Flynn, a reluctant me and a repulsively cheerful Gabes on up the trail towards the top of the waterfall.

The trail narrowed as it ascended through a small pine forest at one point and all we could see for a bit, apart from the track, was the trees. My mind went twisting like ivy around their rough thick trunks; roaming between them like a hungry wolf. I imagined my feelings becoming a ferocious animal, stalking Gabes angrily through the alpine woods.

Eventually we emerged from the forest and climbed up the trail, that glorious sky above us, and all I could hear was Gabes and Dad prattling away to each other, telling themselves how great this was and how lucky we were and how this was the best holiday ever, and I wanted to scream and yell and throw things.

I was so lost in my bad mood that it was a bit of a surprise to suddenly find ourselves at the viewing area at the top of the waterfall. It was a large circular platform, half enclosed by a metal railing, with an information board, a picnic table and a small wooden shelter. There were a couple of men already there – serious hikers, by the looks of them, wearing proper walking gear and carrying a shiny walking pole in each hand – but as we arrived they were shouldering their rucksacks and leaving. One of them said something in German to Dad; Dad smiled, and said 'Afternoon' back.

The men didn't break stride, but the first one called over his shoulder, 'Bad weather is coming! We must get off the mountain.'

They hurried down the track.

Dad frowned and looked at the sky. It was still bright and clear, with hardly a cloud. There was a bit of a breeze, but that was probably coming from the waterfall. He shrugged. 'Wonder which forecast they've been listening to. I guess we shouldn't stay up here *too* long, just in case.'

Still, we needed a breather. Having walked all the way up here we needed a good look at the waterfall from this angle, and there was an information board to read, and then Gabes needed a bit of time to go searching for wildlife in the long grass ...

And suddenly, without warning, the bad weather was upon us. One minute the sky was clear and blue and dazzling; the next a huge grey thundercloud loomed overhead, appearing above the top of the mountain and blotting out the sun like some planet-sized alien mothership from a sinister science fiction movie.

Chapter 7
The Fog

Dad looked up.

'Blimey,' he said. 'Where did that come from? We'd better get going. Or perhaps,' he added, as raindrops the size of marbles began to pelt us, 'we ought to get under cover. Come on!'

It was a good job there was a little shelter at the viewing spot. Not very big, and open to the elements, but at least it had a roof and sides, and there was just about room for the four of us.

'Wow,' Gabes said with a laugh. 'That was sudden!'

I glared at him. I was not having fun and I wasn't going to pretend I was.

'This is rubbish,' Flynn muttered to himself, and I had to agree.

We huddled together, protected from the worst of the rain but still getting spattered as the wind blew raindrops in through the openings in the shelter. Dad opened up his backpack and pulled out our lightweight fleeces; then, as we wriggled into them, he tried to get a game going, but only Gabes joined in. Eventually, as Flynn and I sat in reproachful silence, the game petered out and we waited wordlessly for the rain to stop.

I closed my eyes for a bit and tried to mentally compose an entry for my journal. I wasn't sure exactly what I was going to say about this particular excursion, but I knew I was going to need a few synonyms for 'wet' and 'unpleasant' and 'annoying'. There was something almost hypnotic about the hammering of the rain on the thin wooden roof of the shelter, and I must have gone into some kind of trance or perhaps dozed off, because the next thing I knew, the rain had stopped and Dad was saying, 'Time to go!'

I opened my eyes, feeling uncomfortably cold, and groaned quietly. The cloud had descended and now the viewing point was smothered in a fog so thick that I literally could not see anything outside the shelter.

'What, are you serious?' said Flynn, aghast.

'Well, we can't stay up here all day!' Dad was trying to face the situation with his usual cheerfulness, but he looked uneasy, and suddenly I felt scared. I got to my feet and put my hand in his. Gabes was already clinging to the other one. 'Flynn, take Izzy's hand,' Dad added.

'What?' Flynn said indignantly.

'Or Gabes's. It doesn't matter which, but take one of them. We don't want anyone getting lost up here.' I didn't know when I'd last heard Dad sounding so serious, and that worried me even more. I tightened my grip and moved in close to him.

'OK,' Dad said, doing his best to sound light-hearted and failing miserably. 'This is an adventure, isn't it? Something to tell everyone back home!'

We squeezed out of the shelter and looked around. Apart from the shelter and each other, we could see nothing but grey whiteness. The roar of the nearby waterfall sounded somehow muffled and distant, and it was hard to tell where it was coming from.

'Which way?' said Flynn, his voice coming out almost as a whisper.

'This way, I think,' said Dad, his voice full of false confidence, as he led us forward and straight into the railings. 'Ah,' he went on. 'Well, now, let's see … If we follow these round, we'll find ourselves at the steps.'

We shuffled slowly along the curve of the railings. It seemed to take forever, but eventually we reached a gap.

'Here we are!' said Gabes, with a fake brightness to match Dad's.

I scowled at him – or, at least, I scowled through the fog in his general direction. 'Which way do we go now?' I asked, as we cautiously descended the steps.

'Downhill, of course,' Flynn said scornfully.

I scowled towards him as well. If that was the sort of contribution he was going to make, he could go back to sticking on his headphones and being quiet, as far as I was concerned.

'Can you tell which way is downhill in this fog?' I snapped.

'Of course,' he said, even more contemptuously. 'It's this way.' He turned and began to lead us, but after a moment he stopped, and said, 'Oh.'

'Yeah, *oh*,' I agreed sarcastically. Without any visual cues, it was harder to tell up from down than you might think.

'OK, everybody keep calm,' said Dad, sounding slightly panicked. 'Let's just work this out. We came up the trail and turned ... left, didn't we? So that means we need to turn right once we're out of the viewing area.'

'We're already out of the viewing area,' I pointed out.

'Just be quiet for a moment, Izzy,' Dad said, which I thought was rather unfair considering that I'd hardly said anything all day. 'Now ... let's see ... we followed the railings round ... we came out on the downhill side ... um ... So that must mean it's ... this way!' he declared, sounding suddenly self-assured again. 'Come on! We'll go one behind the other. I'll go first. Gabes, take my hand and follow me. Then Izzy; then Flynn at the back. Don't let go of each other's hands—'

I couldn't help myself. 'What – I have to hold Gabes's hand?'

'Don't start, Izzy!' Dad said.

'What? I—'

'Izzy, we are *lost*. On a *mountain*. In the *fog*. This is too serious a situation for you to start playing silly games about not wanting to hold hands with your brothers!'

'I wasn't—'

'*Enough*, Izzy!'

In the quietness of the fog, the silence that followed felt unreal. For a second, it was as if the whole world had gone away, leaving the four of us stranded without sound, surrounded by nothingness. There was a burning inside me that might have been anger or shame, and my face felt red and flushed. Dad's words hung in the air.

Then Gabes piped up. 'How lost are we, Dad?'

'Mate! Don't worry!' Immediately, Dad was all solicitous. 'We'll be fine! We just need to work as a team. Come on – everyone join hands. Let's get going.'

The silence was broken and the tension lifted a little. But something still burned inside me, as we began to edge down the trail – or what we hoped was the trail.

Dad wasn't taking any chances. He edged forward, testing the ground with his front foot as he went. Slowly, slowly, we felt our way downhill, holding tight to one another's hands. Step by step; centimetre by centimetre.

After what seemed like a thousand such steps, Dad stopped suddenly. 'Oh,' he said, surprised. Through the white blanket of the fog I could just about make out the trunk of a tree, right in front of him. 'This isn't right ... '

'We came up through some trees, though, didn't we?'
Flynn said.

'Fair point,' Dad agreed. 'We did. The track got
narrower, didn't it? But – where is the track? Can you see
it, anyone?'

'I think we've wandered off it a bit,' Flynn answered.
'But I should think we can find it again. If we just ease a
little to the left on the way down ... '

They carried on talking about it, but I stopped listening.
I just wanted the adults to sort things out and get us back
to the van safely.

It was only later that I realized how weird that was –
Flynn and Dad having a grown-up conversation. Like
equals. Dad properly listening, and Flynn properly
talking. Flynn being an adult.

After much discussion we got moving again, working
our slow way down the mountainside. Step by step;
centimetre by centimetre. For what seemed like hours we
edged our way down, Dad and Flynn taking it in turns to
lead the way. I got colder and hungrier. The fog left little
droplets of water on our fleeces, and chilled our faces.

Evening began to fall.

That was when I started to get really scared. It began
to feel like we were going to be lost in this fog and this
encroaching darkness forever. We carried on until the

murky whiteness was replaced by the dark grey of the
twilight shadows, and the darkness swallowed us up.

We stopped. There was a moment's silence.

'What do we do now?' asked Flynn.

'I – ' Dad began. He stopped.

'We can't just wait out here all night,' Flynn said.

'I don't think it's safe to go any further, mate,' Dad said quietly.

'Don't you have a torch in your backpack?'

'I don't think a torch is going to be much good in this fog—'

'It's worth a try!'

There was a sound of unzipping, and fumbling, and Dad's voice said, 'Here.'

A beam of light leaped from Flynn's hand. 'See?' he said, as it lit up the trunk of a tree, just a metre or so away. 'The fog's lifting! Come on!'

We edged forward again, through the trees. Visibility still wasn't good, but it was better than it had been earlier. I could hear my heart pounding in my chest as we walked slowly, carefully forward.

And then Flynn lost his footing and stumbled against a tree. The light from the torch flickered and dimmed to a glow. 'No!' he yelled in fury.

I heard the slap of the torch against his hand; saw the glow fade further to a sudden pinpoint in the darkness.

'No!' Flynn howled again, as if this last obstacle had broken him. I saw the pinpoint draw back and shoot into the darkness, and just as I realized Flynn had flung the torch away in anger and frustration, I heard two noises.

The first was a *clank*, as if the torch had struck something large and hollow and metallic.

The second came a moment later, from inside the large hollow metallic thing. It was a sound I never, ever thought I'd be happy to hear, and certainly not as happy as it made me at that moment:

'eeeeeeeeeeee!'

The Travelling Travises!

Sorry for the radio silence – it's not always easy finding a Wi-Fi connection up a Swiss mountain! And that's where we've been for the past week!

I don't have a good enough connection to post photos right now, but don't worry – they'll be online soon! And we've got some amazing shots to share with you! The adventures have been awesome!

No shots from our last day here, though – we got lost up a mountain in the fog! Or, at least, Flynn, Izzy, Gabes and I (Martin) did. Vikks and Tyrone took the sensible option of Swiss chocolate and a movie! Still, we came together in a crisis! I was proud of the kids – and it's at times like that you notice how grown-up your eldest is getting!

Martin, Vikki, Flynn, Izzy, Gabes & Tyrone

Chapter 8
The Harbour

Moments after Tyrone started ululating, the van's interior light went on and we groped our grateful way inside.

Mum hadn't even noticed we were missing. She and Tyrone had ended up watching not one but two movies, and then they'd both fallen asleep until Flynn's furious but fortunate flinging of the torch had woken them. When she heard what had happened to us, though, she got really stressed. So of course Dad tried to make out it had all been some big adventure.

'An adventure? Anything could have happened, Martin! Anything! You were on a mountain – a *mountain* – in the dark!'

'Vikks, sweetheart! Relax! In a few days you'll look back at this and laugh!'

'Don't you *dare* tell me I will laugh about this, Martin Travis. Don't you *dare!*'

Suddenly, they were locked into an escalating argument. Dad was trying to reassure Mum, while Mum was getting crosser and crosser. Dad started to panic – I could see it in his eyes – and tried harder. The harder he tried, the angrier Mum got.

It was horrible. I'd been scared, and cold, and now we

were inside all I wanted to do was drink my hot chocolate and curl up in my bed, knowing that Mum and Dad were looking after me. Instead, this was happening.

Then Flynn spoke.

'Mum – it's OK. We're safe now.'

It was the weirdest thing; he didn't raise his voice at all, and yet somehow it cut through the loudness of my parents and stopped them in their tracks.

Mum turned to him, and he stood up and said again, 'It's OK, Mum,' and gave her a hug. For just a moment, it felt like he was the adult and she was a scared little girl. There was a pause; everything felt still and safe.

Then the bravado left Dad's face, and he put his arms around Mum and Flynn, and Mum's shoulders started shaking like she was crying. Gabes and I flung ourselves at them, and Tyrone hurled himself at the huddle and clung on like a limpet, and then the six of us were standing there holding each other as if we were the only things that mattered in the world.

And just for a minute, we were.

I don't know how long we stayed in that hug, but eventually I felt Tyrone burrow into the middle, squeezing between Mum and Dad, and his voice, muffled and indistinct, broke the silence. 'Can we have hot chocolate now?'

Everyone laughed as we let go. Mum stepped back, wiping her face.

'Of course we can, mate,' Dad said, reaching for the saucepan. 'Do you want to get the milk out for me?'

Flynn popped his headphones on and sat down.

Gabes looked at me and grinned, and I almost grinned back. Then I remembered that it was all his fault. If it hadn't been for him, we wouldn't have been here to get stuck on the wretched mountain in the stupid fog in the first place. So I looked away, and went and got my notebook out, while we waited for Dad to serve up the hot chocolate.

* * *

As we left Switzerland and headed down through Italy, things felt somehow different. Flynn didn't exactly give up his headphones, but he spent less time with them jammed on his head, and more time joining in with things. He even started to take his turn travelling in the front of the van. Mum and Dad, meanwhile, and especially Dad, started treating him more like a grown-up – asking his opinion on things, listening seriously when he made a suggestion. It was as if those hours in the fog had made him grow up a bit – or maybe they'd made Dad see something in him that had been there for a while. It felt as if a cloud had lifted, somehow.

My own personal cloud, however, was still there. Gabes was relentlessly cheerful, jabbering away when I wanted time to myself, and ... and was just generally *annoying*. I could have done without him around. Every time we stopped I went to the back of the van to try to find my own space, just to be rid of him – reading one of the library books I'd brought with me, or writing in my journal. Mum and Dad have always encouraged my reading and writing, so it gave me the perfect excuse to tell on him:

'Mum! Gabes is bothering me when I'm trying to read!'

'Come on, Gabes, stop disturbing your sister.'

'But – I was just trying to show her that bird, up there! I think it's an osprey—'

'Gabes ... Leave her alone, now.'

To be honest, half the time I wasn't even reading – just lost in thought, with a book open in front of me. But it gave me a cold, burning satisfaction to see the confusion on his face when I brushed him off.

Down along the Italian coast we drove until, at dusk, we arrived at a little fishing village. We pulled up at our campsite by the coast road and I drifted off, lulled to sleep by the sound of the lapping waves.

Next morning, I was rudely awakened by Gabes. 'Izzy! Izzy! Wake up! We're going fishing!'

I scowled up into his excited, puppyish face. 'So? You don't have to wake me up and yell about it.'

Deflated, Gabes tried again. 'But you have to get up. We're going straight after breakfast.'

'All right,' I grumbled. 'Keep your hair on.'

Amazingly, I was the last one out of bed. Even Flynn was already dressed and when I joined the family at the makeshift breakfast table Mum had set up outside in the morning sunshine, he was chatting to her with something that almost resembled excitement.

'Yeah, I don't know what woke me early, but you were all still fast asleep, so I went for a stroll into the village and I met this guy called Massimo. He's going off to study English at university in September, so he was really pleased to get a bit of practice by speaking to me, and then he told me that his dad has a fishing boat and might take us out for a trip.'

I stared at Flynn, not quite able to believe that this was the same monosyllabic big brother who'd spent most of the trip silent and plugged into his headphones.

'So when I came back I talked to Dad about it—'

'And I thought it was a great idea!' Dad cut in. 'I'm proud of you, mate – setting up something like that for us. He's given you a good price too. It's going to be one of the highlights of the trip, I reckon.'

'Yeah,' said Gabes enthusiastically. 'It'll be great!'

'It won't if you spend the whole time throwing up over the side of the boat,' I muttered.

'eeeee**eeeeee!**' went Tyrone.

'Mate! What's wrong?'

'I don't – *eeeee* – I don't – *eeeeeee* – I don't *wanna* go out on a boat!'

'That's all right,' Mum said. 'I don't particularly feel a need to go, either. What say you and I go and explore the village? Look!' She pointed across the road to where row upon row of brightly-painted cottages clustered together on the hillside, illuminated by the golden morning sun. Tyrone looked at them and nodded.

'That's settled, then,' said Dad. 'Let's get through breakfast and down to the harbour!'

The harbour, too, was quaint and pretty. We entered through a stone arch that looked very old and much too grand for such a little place, as if in ancient times the village had been much bigger and more important than it was now and this was all that was left of its former glory. The painted wooden jetty looked as if it had been scrubbed clean by a legion of house-proud villagers. A small handful of boats bobbed gently on the water, and on one of the larger ones a couple of suntanned Italians were getting ready for a morning's fishing.

'There's Massimo,' said Flynn, and waved. The younger of the two men grinned and waved back.

Mum and Tyrone stood on the pier and watched as we scrambled on board. I guess we weren't the first tourists Massimo and his dad had taken out for a trip, because from somewhere they produced life jackets for all of us.

I headed up to the front of the boat as they were getting it ready and looked out across the water, noting the way the golden morning sunlight scattered silver sparkles across the sea, and imagining I could see dancers in the water. I was just getting nicely lost in my own thoughts when – of course – Gabes came up behind me.

'This is going to be fun, isn't it?' he said, with a kind of bright desperation for attention.

I'd had enough. As if it wasn't sufficient that Gabes had landed us all on a holiday that nobody but Dad wanted to go on, I couldn't even get a bit of time in the privacy of my own imagination without him pestering me. So I said, 'It'll be a lot more fun if you don't keep bothering me.'

Gabes looked back at me as if I'd slapped him, and his eyes started glistening. I raised my own eyes to the sky; the last thing I needed was him getting all weepy and whiny. But when I looked back at him, I saw something that I simply hadn't expected. Gabes's expression was set rock-hard. He stood up as tall as he could, took a step towards me, pushed his face right into mine, and said in a tone that was pure frost, 'Why are you so horrible?'

My mouth fell open. 'What?'

'Why are you so horrible?' Gabes repeated, and this time his voice trembled. 'You've been mean to me all summer! You're *always* mean to me! I'm trying to be friendly, and you're just nothing but nasty, all the time!'

I felt indignation rise within me. 'Me, horrible? That's rich, coming from you! It's your fault we're on this stupid holiday in the first place! If you hadn't given Dad that silly idea about sleeping arrangements, he'd have given up on it!'

Gabes's eyes narrowed furiously. 'This *isn't* a stupid holiday! It's the best one we've ever been on, and if you weren't so selfish and ... and *mean*, you'd see that! Look at all the things we've done! Look at *that*!'

Gabes gestured back across the harbour to where the village stood on the hillside, and then swept his arm out across the water. 'We've never been anywhere like this! Never seen anything like this! How can you not want to be here? How can you wish you were at home watching TV? Well, *I* want to be here. I want to see new things, and do new things with Mum and Dad and Flynn and Tyrone! But not you, Izzy! I wish you weren't my sister! I *hate* you!'

I stood, stunned, feeling the boat move under me and feeling as if my whole world had shifted somehow. Gabes had never spoken to me like this before. Gabes had never spoken to *anyone* like this before.

My mouth quivered, searching for something to say, some clever response that would put him in his place. But as I groped, he spat the words out again, loud and vicious:

'I hate you!'

Fumbling with his life jacket, he turned away and half-stomped, half-ran to the point where we'd embarked. He tore the life jacket off, flung it on the deck and leaped on to the jetty.

Mum took a step towards him as he marched towards her, wiping his eyes violently. She bent down, exchanged a few words, and then put her arms around him.

From the back of the boat, Dad cast a puzzled look at Mum. She made a 'don't worry' kind of gesture, and – with a glance at me that made me go cold and numb inside – took Gabes by one hand and Tyrone by the other, and turned back along the jetty towards the village.

Dad looked at me and I looked away, something like shame burning through me. It wasn't my fault that Gabes had decided to go off on one. It wasn't my fault that he couldn't hear the truth.

But as Massimo and his dad cast off, and the boat headed out into the blue waters, something inside me whispered darkly that it was. It was all my fault.

The Travelling Travises!

Flynn organized a fishing trip for us!

He, Izzy and I headed out to catch our tea while Vikks, Gabes and Tyrone took a stroll around the prettiest little village any of us have ever seen!

Days like this don't come along very often!

Martin, Vikki, Flynn, Izzy, Gabes & Tyrone

Chapter 9
The Boat

The gentle putt-putt-putt of the engine as we sailed out into open water sounded somehow accusing. It was as if the boat was echoing my thoughts: *It's all your fault. It's all your fault. It's all your fault.*

I sat in the bow, right at the front of the boat, staring out with blank eyes. Gabes was right. I'd never seen anything quite like this before, and yet I couldn't properly see it now. I should have been taking in the sights: the sunlight, the water, the seabirds and the other fishing boats in the distance. I should have been finding words and phrases, working out how to paint pictures in the imagination with my writing, to show my reader what all this was like. But all I could really see was Gabes's face. The tears in his eyes and the hurt and hatred in his expression.

It felt like there were two rats fighting inside my stomach. One was cursing Gabes, telling me he'd brought all this upon himself by enabling this holiday. Telling me he was annoying and stupid and deserved everything he got.

The other was cursing me. It was telling me that all Gabes was guilty of was enthusiasm. That he was right – I had been selfish to not want this holiday, selfish and wrong. We'd been having fun, but it would have been more fun if it wasn't for me. And I should be having fun now – casting a line over the side, trying to catch a fish, getting caught up in Dad's excitement. But I couldn't. I couldn't because I'd driven Gabes off. I was a horrible person.

I don't know how long I'd sat there with the rats fighting inside me, when I heard footsteps approaching. I stiffened as someone knelt down behind me and an arm slipped around my shoulders. The last thing I wanted right now was Dad trying to cheer me up by pretending everything was fine when it clearly wasn't.

But it wasn't Dad.

'Want to talk about it?' It was Flynn.

Oddly, I did. But I couldn't. I opened my mouth and tried to speak, but nothing came out.

'It's OK,' Flynn said quietly. 'I'm guessing you've had a row with Gabes, right?'

I nodded, mutely.

'Was the row your fault, do you think?'

I nodded, squeezing my eyes shut in a vain attempt to stop the tears from trickling out.

Flynn gave my shoulder a gentle rub. 'Don't worry,' he said. 'You know Gabes. I don't think I've ever met anyone as easy-going and quick to forgive as our little brother.'

And with that, the floodgates opened.

Flynn was right: Gabes never held a grudge. He never got ratty or irritable. He never took his bad feelings out on the rest of us, never blamed anyone unfairly, never did anything deliberately hurtful. I'd taken advantage of that; I'd taken my own bad moods out on someone who never fought back. I'd blamed him, just because I could. I'd pushed him, and pushed him, and pushed him, certain he'd never push back. I'd done the impossible: I'd made Gabes furious. I'd hurt him so much he hated me. And now I was crying as if I'd never stop; howling as if my heart would break.

I heard more footsteps approaching and felt Flynn shift position as if waving someone away. Then I felt his arms around me. He said nothing; just held me as I sobbed and sobbed at the knowledge of how mean I'd been.

By the time the tears stopped coming, my throat hurt and the skin around my eyes stung saltily. I wriggled out of Flynn's embrace and sat up, wiping my wet face, remorseful and exhausted.

Flynn looked down at me. 'Better?' he said.

I looked inside myself and realized that, yes, I did feel better. I felt drained and empty, but much calmer. I sniffed and gulped, and found that I could speak now, but I didn't know what to say.

Flynn smiled. 'We'll sort it out when we get back to shore,' he said, standing and holding out his hand to help me up. 'In the meantime, let's go and catch some fish.'

* * *

That day, I rediscovered two people.

Firstly, I rediscovered Flynn. It was as if the big brother I remembered from when I was younger – the one who used to give me rides on his back, who used to laugh and joke and play with me – had come back, bigger and brighter than before. It felt as if he'd sealed himself into a chrysalis when his voice broke, and now he'd wriggled out of it again, transformed into a proper grown-up – or, at least, someone closer to a grown-up than a child. I supposed that really he'd begun wriggling out of the chrysalis when we were up the mountain, and maybe he was going to be wriggling out of it for a while. But what mattered was that we'd reconnected.

Secondly, I rediscovered myself. I don't know what had turned me into the bitter, harsh girl I'd been over the last few weeks, but whatever it was, I felt as if I'd cried it all out, safe in my big brother's arms. And now I was ready to be a big sister to my little brother again.

Maybe that was it. Maybe when I'd lost Flynn to the chrysalis, I'd somehow lost part of myself. Who knows?

I managed to enjoy myself as we fished, though there was still a hollowness inside me. I couldn't help feeling that Gabes would have loved this, and it was my fault he wasn't here. But as I stood on the deck, battling with my fishing rod, it felt as if the salt spray was washing me clean, and the fresh sea air was blowing away something that had dwelt inside me for too long.

All too soon, we turned and headed back with our catch. My heart sank as I thought about facing Gabes.

As the boat putt-putted into the harbour, I moved closer to Flynn, and he put his arm around me reassuringly.

There they were, on the jetty as we pulled in – Mum and Gabes and Tyrone. Standing, waiting for us. I looked down at the little plastic bucket Massimo had given me and at my catch of six slender silver fish. I took another bucket from the stack by the motor, and slipped three of them into it. Then, a bucket in each hand, I stepped off the boat and walked towards Gabes.

'Here,' I said, holding one out to him. 'I caught these for you.'

Gabes looked at the sardines, and then at me, his face expressionless. He nodded, reached out his hand and took the bucket. Then he pointed back along the harbour wall and said quietly, 'I found some lizards. Do you want to see them?'

I felt tears springing to my eyes again, and swallowed hard. 'I'd love to,' I said, and as he turned away, I followed.

The Travelling Travises!

Wow! Has it been six weeks already?

We've had the most amazing time! Hope you've enjoyed the blog posts – especially the pictures! We've got lots more of those to show our friends and family when we get back!

Right now, though, we're off for our last night out before we head home! And where better to spend our final evening than in glamorous Paris!

See you soon!

Martin, Vikki, Flynn, Izzy, Gabes & Tyrone

Chapter 10
The Return

We had a barbecue on the beach. Dad grilled the fish we'd caught, and – well, I think they were the best thing I'd ever tasted. I sat between Flynn and Gabes, and though we didn't chat much, everything felt OK again. Better than OK.

I looked at my journal that evening, and couldn't believe it when I realized that almost everything I'd written had been negative. Complaints about Gabes, moaning about the things that had gone wrong. Nothing – or virtually nothing – about all the amazing things we'd seen and done. It was as if I'd been trying to blank them out. I read what I had written about our week in the Swiss Alps. All those astonishing experiences, squashed into a single slightly begrudging paragraph, and then pages and pages about the disaster of getting lost in the fog.

Thankfully, Mum and Dad have been taking photographs all the way through the holiday. I think I might ask if they can print out some of the best ones, and I can make a display on one wall of my bedroom.

We had more astonishing experiences over the last bit of our holiday. And, yes, I'm going to squash those into a single paragraph too – not because I didn't enjoy them, but because I didn't feel like writing much in my journal after the fishing trip. I felt that I'd poisoned it, by writing all those horrible things about poor Gabes, and that the best way to appreciate the rest of the holiday was to put the journal aside and just enjoy myself. Don't worry, I haven't given up writing. It's just that next time I go on holiday with my family I want to write about the good things, not the bad.

And actually, there's too much to fit into a single paragraph anyway. Too much for a whole book! There's so much that I could say about the ruins of Pompeii, where history and time seemed to have just stopped; about the beauties of Rome and Florence; about the Mediterranean coastline and the golden beaches; about the towns and the cities and the countryside. And, of course, about Paris, where we walked along the Champs-Élysées, and climbed the Eiffel Tower, and stood on the steps of Montmartre at night. But in any case, those weren't the very best bits.

The very best bit was, quite simply, being with my family. For all their faults and foibles. For all that Gabes still winds me up sometimes. For all that Tyrone can be irritating, and Flynn can be sullen and surly (he still hasn't finished emerging from that chrysalis, after all). And for all that Dad can be stupidly enthusiastic, and ridiculously optimistic, and for all that Mum sometimes holds her tongue when she should speak, and lets Dad drag us into scrapes when she should put her foot down, and for all that she occasionally worries too much. For all that and more, they're my family, and I wouldn't be without them. No matter what.

Did you notice something, by the way, about the last photo on Dad's blog? The one taken in Paris?

We're all smiling. All of us: big, genuine, happy smiles. I take back what I said, way back at the beginning, about Dad's ideas. This holiday was, by far, the best idea he's ever, ever had. I'm only sorry I didn't realize it sooner.

* * *

We spent two days in Paris, and made the most of every second, because we knew that our holiday was drawing to an end. And on our final morning, we got up early and made for the ferry. Gabes was seasick on the crossing again, and while it would be a stretch to say I was happy to look after him, I did it gladly. He's my brother, after all. And this time I had Flynn to help me.

From Dover we headed towards the motorway, and by mid-afternoon we were pulling up outside our house, tired and happy.

That was when Mum let out a horrified gasp and clutched at Dad's arm.

'Martin! Look!'

It took us a moment to realize what she was pointing at. And then we got it. The upstairs window – Mum and Dad's bedroom window – was open. Wide open.

'I closed it,' Mum said shakily. 'I went round shutting all the windows and checking the doors before we left!'

We looked at one another, knowing what this must mean.

'I'll go in,' said Dad. 'You stay here. The burglar might still be in the house.'

'I'll come,' said Flynn. 'You might need help.'

'eeeeee**eeeeee**!' went Tyrone.

'Shhhhh!' hissed the rest of us simultaneously, and Tyrone was so astonished that he shushed.

We stood nervously behind Dad as he walked to the front door and slipped his key silently into the lock. But before he could turn it – the door opened.

'Aaargh!' said Dad.

'Aaargh!' said Mum.

'Aaargh!' said Flynn and me and Gabes and Tyrone.

'Aaargh!' said Aunty Fi.

'Fi!' Dad breathed, almost collapsing with relief. 'What are you doing here?'

'I might ask you the same thing!' Aunty Fi said. 'I wasn't expecting you till this evening!'

'We got an early ferry,' Dad said. 'What about you? We thought you were a burglar!'

Aunty Fi smiled. 'It'd have served you right if I was!' she said. 'Honestly, Martin – what did you think you were doing, putting a picture on the Internet that clearly showed your house, right next to a blog post that said you were going away for six weeks? Have you no idea about Internet security? I thought I'd better come and house-sit, before every burglar in the area decided to drop by!'

Dad went pale. 'Oh,' he said. 'I didn't think of that.'

Aunty Fi shook her head. 'Of course not,' she said. 'You never do think! It's like that time when we were kids, and – oh, never mind. It's a good job I'm still here to look out for you, that's all. Anyway, let me put the kettle on, and you can tell me all about it. Was it a good holiday?'

'It was great!' said Gabes. 'The best holiday ever.'

'I wouldn't have missed it for anything,' said Flynn, making Aunty Fi raise her eyebrows in mock surprise.

I looked at Dad. He'd gone pink and was grinning from ear to ear. Mum was holding his hand and looking proud, and Tyrone was snuggling into them both.

I looked up at Flynn, too – my own big brother – and at Gabes, and they both looked back at me. Suddenly I felt I was home in more ways than one.

'What about you, Izzy?' Aunty Fi asked. 'What sort of holiday was it for you?'

I thought back over everything we'd done, everything we'd seen, and more importantly, how the last six weeks had brought us all together, and I knew there was only one answer.

'The holiday of a lifetime,' I said.

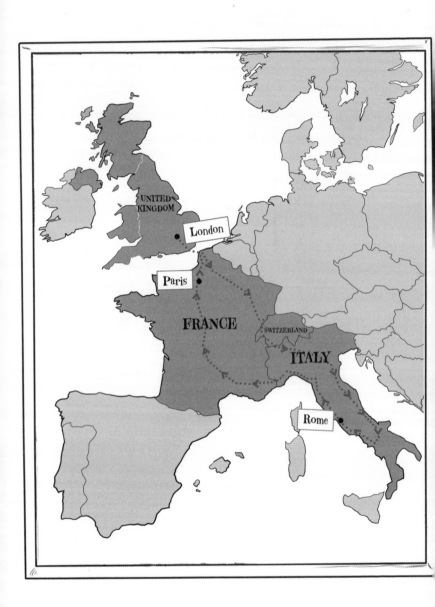